the orchard

First Edition, April 1991
The title of the Spanish edition is *Los árboles frutales*.

All inquiries should be addressed to:
Barron's Educational Series, Inc.
250 Wireless Boulevard
Hauppauge, New York 11788

Library of Congress Catalog Card No. 91-7749

International Standard Book No. 0-8120-4710-9

Library of Congress Cataloging-in-Publication Data
Sánchez, Isidro.
[Arboles frutales. English]
The orchard / I. Sánchez, C. Peris — 1st ed.
p. cm. — (Discovering nature)
Translation of: Los árboles frutales.
Summary: Explains about fruit trees, what they produce, and how they grow.
ISBN 0-8120-4710-9
1. Fruit-culture—Juvenile literature. 2. Fruit trees—Juvenile literature. 3. Fruit—Juvenile literature. [1. Fruit culture. 2. Fruit trees. 3. Fruit.] I. Peris, C. (Carme). II. Title. III. Series: Sánchez, I. (Isidro). Discovering nature.
SB357.2.R5813 1991
634—dc20

91-7749
CIP
AC

Legal Deposit: B. 14.946-91
Printed in Spain
1234 987654321

discovering nature

the orchard

I. Sánchez
C. Peris

New York • Toronto • Sydney

We live near an orchard, so we can go to visit it often. It's fun to see how the fruit trees grow.

In early spring we watch the farmers plow the fields and fertilize the soil.

The tiny fruit trees are arranged in the ground in neat rows. They are tied to stakes that help them grow straight.

As the trees grow, they are trimmed. Some branches are cut to make the other branches grow stronger.

Before the fruit appears, the flowers bloom. The fruit trees look very pretty then.

In the summer and fall, when the fruit is ripe, it is time for the harvest. Pears and apples are delicious to eat. They have seeds in the center part, which is called the core.

This cherry tree has a lot of beautiful red cherries. Like plums, peaches, and apricots, cherries have only one hard pit inside them.

Some trees produce nuts—like almonds, walnuts, pecans, and hazelnuts. They are good to eat, too.

Many kinds of fruit are dried and packed in plastic bags or boxes. Did you know that prunes are dried plums?

Fruit can be shipped in refrigerated trucks and stored in cool warehouses. That means we are able to eat fresh fruit all year.

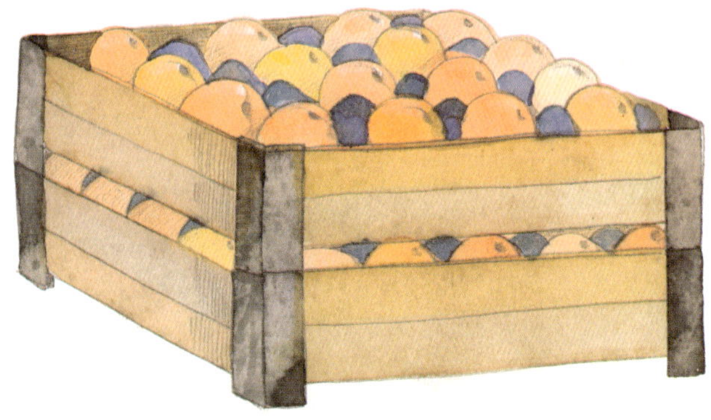

In the market there is also fruit that comes from all over the world—mangoes, papayas, kiwis, and many others.

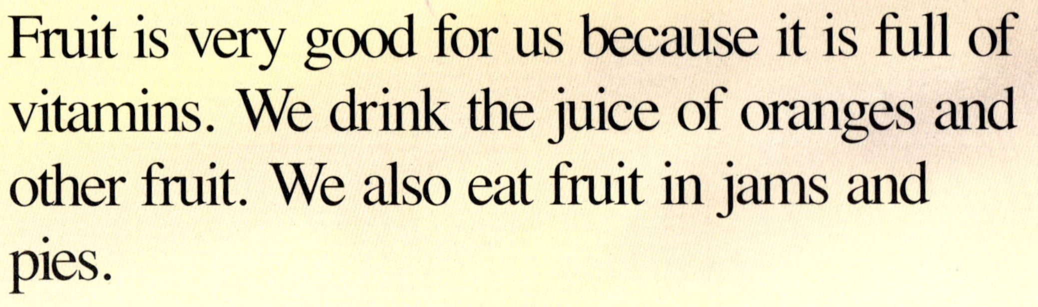

Fruit is very good for us because it is full of vitamins. We drink the juice of oranges and other fruit. We also eat fruit in jams and pies.

We must always wash fruit well if we eat it fresh.

THE ORCHARD

Fruit trees, a wonderful discovery

For children who live in large cities (as well as for many adults), food is something that is purchased at the market; its actual origin is rarely considered. Because of this, a child's first contact with fruit-producing trees can be a wonderful, often magical, discovery.

The amazing fact that oranges, pears, cherries, and apples hang from trees is the insight parents and teachers can use to help children progress in their knowledge of nature and its gifts.

Flowers and fruit

Children are astonished and delighted when they can eat fruit that is picked directly from the tree that produces it. This encourages them to question many things and provides an opportunity to teach them that flowers are an important stage in the life cycle of plants—not simply a decorative element in nature. Fruit, in fact, develops from the fertilized flower; and the remains of that flower can still be seen at the base of certain kinds of fruit (apples, pears, etc.). The role of the bee in transferring the powdery pollen to the sticky tip of the pistil can be explained to slightly older children.

Different trees, different fruit

Opening a pear, an apple, a plum, etc., can provide further revelations for children. For instance, they can learn that the purpose of the fruit is to attract the animals that will pick it, eat it, and scatter the seeds on the soil, where it will germinate to create new trees.

Different kinds of fruit use different strategies to preserve their seeds and appeal to animals. For instance, children can be taught that there are trees that produce fleshy fruit (apples, oranges, etc.) and others that produce large, edible seeds within hard, protective shells (almonds, hazelnuts, etc.).

Kinds of fleshy fruit

Cutting an apple or a pear in half lengthwise reveals that in this kind of fleshy fruit, several small seeds are found in several small chambers. On the other hand, fleshy fruit such as peaches or plums have a single, central seed. Use a nutcracker to break open the pit of a peach and show the children the almond-like seed that is concealed within.

How different apples are from oranges! This simple observation can be used to introduce the wonderful structure of the citrus fruits (oranges, grapefruit, lemons, etc.), which have hundreds of little bladders full of juice. Grapes and berries are different types of fleshy fruit.

The "juiceless" fruit

The seed within a peach, plum, or apricot pit can be used to introduce the almond, walnut, pecan, and other nut-bearing trees. You might also mention that the legumes (beans and peas) also produce edible seeds. Break open the pods of some fresh beans or peas and look at the seeds inside. Then enrich the lesson by letting the children plant some dried limas. Make sure the containers are watered every few days and that they have adequate drainage.

To encourage curiosity

Children can learn about fruit trees in many ways: through the study of their cultivation, by knowing about the products derived from various fruit (grapes/wine, apples/cider, jams, etc.), by enjoying and becoming aware of the nourishing value of natural fruit (which is rich in vitamins). Properly presented, all of these facts and experiences will contribute to the child's education and further stimulate curiosity.